THE PORTAGE POETRY SERIES

SERIES TITLES

Cuttings
Hannah Dow

Where Babies Come From
Ori Fienberg

Forgive the Animal
Sarah Pape

Love as Invasive Species
Ellen Kombiyil

They Were Horrible Cooks
Allison Whittenberg

The New Life
Wendy Wisner

Table with Burning Candle
Julia Paul

A Bright Wound
Sarah A. Etlinger

The Velvet Book
Rae Gouirand

Listening to Mars
Sally Ashton

Glitter City
Bonnie Jill Emanuel

The Trouble with Being a Childless Only Child
Michelle Meyer

Happy Everything
Caitlin Cowan

Dear Lo
Brady Bove

Sadness of the Apex Predator
Dion O'Reilly

Do Not Feed the Animal
Hikari Miya

The Watching Sky
Judy Brackett Crowe

Let It Be Told in a Single Breath
Russell Thorburn

The Blue Divide
Linda Nemec Foster

Lake, River, Mountain
Mark B. Hamilton

Talking Diamonds
Linda Nemec Foster

Poetic People Power
Tara Bracco (ed.)

The Green Vault Heist
David Salner

There is a Corner of Someplace Else
Camden Michael Jones

Everything Waits
Jonathan Graham

We Are Reckless
Christy Prahl

Always a Body
Molly Fuller

Cuttings

poems

Hannah Dow

CORNERSTONE PRESS
UNIVERSITY OF WISCONSIN-STEVENS POINT

Cornerstone Press, Stevens Point, Wisconsin 54481
Copyright © 2024 Hannah Dow
www.uwsp.edu/cornerstone

Printed in the United States of America by
Point Print and Design Studio, Stevens Point, Wisconsin

Library of Congress Control Number: 2024942452
ISBN: 978-1-960329-57-8

Cornerstone Press titles are produced in courses and internships offered by the
Department of English at the University of Wisconsin–Stevens Point.

DIRECTOR & PUBLISHER
Dr. Ross K. Tangedal

EXECUTIVE EDITORS
Jeff Snowbarger, Freesia McKee

EDITORIAL DIRECTOR
Ellie Atkinson

SENIOR EDITORS
Brett Hill, Grace Dahl

PRESS STAFF
Carolyn Czerwinski, Elyse Edens, Allison Lange, Sophie McPherson, Kylie
Newton, Kacey Schmidt, Ava Willett

For my mother,
who cultivated this love of the written word.

ALSO BY HANNAH DOW:

Rosarium: Poems

Contents

III.

IV.

…a future possible self, which is a kind of mother.
—Rachel Zucker, MOTHERs

*What else hurts you, the mother says
and the daughter says, What about you.*

—Hayan Charara

Mycorrhiza

A forest, like a family, is greater
than the sum of its parts. Or:
one tree cannot be replaced
with another. Beneath,

a mother tree always makes room,
adjusts roots to clear space
for her offspring. The infection
she gives them is nurture,

survival. Even in death, a mother knows
best: she sends you into the world
as her seedling. Knows you
will not make it out unfelled.

I.

My Mother Tries to Teach Me About Faith

1.

You begin with the story
of St. Eulalia, a girl not unlike me—
slow to speak and tortured
by her own convictions.
I tell you I would give anything
to summon a snowstorm
when I feel afraid
or a dove to fly from my mouth,
because silence is never enough.

2.

You begin with the story
of the disciples—how, when they felt
a heavy wind toss the water beneath
their boat, they called out
to Jesus to save them, but when
he walked toward them
on the water, in their fear,
the disciples mistook him for a ghost.
I tell you a ghost comes to visit me
at night. A ghost whose name
sounds like birdsong, like wind
when it turns itself over water.

3.

You begin with the story
of the mustard seed—how anyone
with just a speck of belief

could tell a mountain to move
and it would. I tell you
this is called *fault-block*—
mountains are moving all around us
whether we tell them to or not.

4.

I begin this poem by mistyping
the word faith, which, without its last letter,
means fact. I've heard so many stories
by now that I've lost the fine thread
of Eulalia's golden hair, the shadow
of the ghost, the single mustard seed
before it even has a chance
to slip through my fingers.

5.

I want to begin with the story
of yesterday—how I saw
a western grebe walk across a lake
with the confidence of a god
who does not believe in winter
even as snow began to fall
around us like words I could never
summon on my own.

Strange Penance

Every house we lived in my mother gutted to the endoskel-
eton. Tore down walls to make new rooms, swapped in win-
dows to trap the sun. Wrecked her knees laying tile. In the
meantime, my brother and I distanced ourselves outside, skip-
ping pebbles, playing house beneath pine trees, sweeping dirt
flat and smooth beneath our feet. Once, I found the rotting
carcass of a trout and wanted to know how it had died on
land, convinced myself I'd killed it with a wayward stone. I
wanted to give it a proper burial, but my mother said *soil is
mercy enough, the earth doesn't need our help to carry, bones and
all, its creatures home.* Still, I wanted to scrape my fingernails
into the backyard's granitic soil, dig my knuckles raw with the
repetition. Pain, the only ritual I knew.

First Flight

When Daedalus warned his son not to fly too close to the sun,
he must have known that a warning, to a child, is as empty
as a liar's promise when what glimmers is, in fact, gold. Surely,
architect of flight that he was, Daedalus would have known
that flying too high would also mean a painful increase in pressure,
the room of a child's ear stretching like a gum-bubble on the brink
of pop. I don't want to imagine Icarus suffering any more
than he must have when he first felt the drip of hot wax on his arm
or saw feathers unleash beneath him like heavy snow.

My first flight, I pressed my palm against the window
and imagined touching the sun as my mother warned
me not to look right at it. But here is how one harm can be traded
for another: through the painful buzzing in my small ears I asked
for water, as if to dissolve the consequence of forgetting
to Q-tip away what I thought was a build-up of too much wax.

My Mother Tries to Teach Me About Language

All things begin with a single word.
This time, the word is a name.

> The time I defile God's name,
> you resolve to put an end to my cursing.

You resolve to put an end to my cursing
by filling my mouth with soap.

> The soap fills my mouth with sweet olive
> and cleans me from the inside out.

To be cleansed from the inside out
is the reason we drink wine at church.

> Now I drink wine to forget the Church,
> rinse my mouth with the blood of its hurt.

I rinse my mouth of blood, forget why I hurt.
It must have begun with a single word.

The Sound

Sometimes I press my ear
against a wall to seek the hum
one might otherwise mistake

for electricity: the yellowjackets who made
an interstitial hive of my childhood
bedroom. Sometimes, they tiptoed

through the sockets, pulsed
through my sleepless nights. I was afraid
of everything, and a life without their poison

was my *never have I ever.* I learned
to paralyze my breath
and tricked myself into believing

that a yellowjacket was just another
lonely child in a raincoat
walking herself to the bus stop,

abuzz in that flight between day and night,
night and day on restless wings.

My Mother Tries to Teach Me How To Draw

I'm drawing this: a man with massive feet
and spindly arms that hula-hoop the waist
of a sleeping woman. I drape a sheet

across her body because he knows she'll
soon grow cold. Next, I pencil an escape
ladder for the man with massive feet,

a second-story window, and the street
beneath. Look, I say—you go red-faced—
a sleeping woman draped in a bedsheet?

You should tell me I've drawn a crime scene,
pick up my reckless pencil and erase
it all—chiefly, the man with massive feet.

Instead, you help me roll my drawing, neat
and snug into a poster tube, embraced
like the sleeping woman draped in her sheet.

You can't predict what happens next. The heat
of a man's gaze as I bend to re-lace
my shoe. That outsized attention. My feet,
my animal instinct for danger: asleep.

After Chloe Honum

My Mother Tries to Teach Me About the Body

The first time I uncover a horseshoe crab
in the sand and study its spiny turtle-shell
and the long point of what is probably not
its tail, you pick it up, revealing
its complex underside—the legs
and legs and gills—I run away, shrieking.

This is the same summer I learn
that if I hold very, very still, I can
almost make myself invisible

to bees. Almost invisible, like the toddler
who, this same summer, stumbles into
your car, leg pinched by the claw of your tire.
Even though the boy is fine, you have nightmares
about his bruises for years. I learn that a bruise
is just the body's way of keeping

everything inside. In my nightmares,
my classmates watch surveillance video of me
showering or changing clothes. They laugh
at all my mismatched parts while I learn
to pinch my body for acne. For fat. Learn to hate
my body in a swimsuit. The sudden

blood. I learn that horseshoe crabs
are evolutionary marvels harvested
to identify contamination within medical supplies.
Most—but not all—survive
this bleeding, and it makes the females
too exhausted to reproduce. The milky

blueness of their blood is something
I would like to have. I know this
the same way I know there is a danger
that lives in my body and I
am the only one who cannot see it.

Bildungsroman

Trumpets without tongues, we wove lilies
into the baskets. When they asked us
what we meant by these, we'd say "mary, mary"
and be still. We lined the baskets on the sill…
—Eleanor Rand Wilner

Trumpets without tongues, we wove lilies
into the shoots of one another's hair.
Light into dark into light, I'd never seen
anything so splendid or straightforward.
Her fingers moved with the unruly
patience only a child can manage,
and I remember how clean
her palms were despite our digging,
gathering. The way she folded stem
over stem, the petals' fragile sheen

into the baskets. When they asked us
to come inside, we obeyed and left everything
behind. When they looked away, we danced
in the kitchen to her father's smoking
songs. She lifted my hands
to her shoulders, the shallow
slope of her neck. Every time I glimpsed
our reflection in the lofty windows,
I knew we were each imagining the other
into others—and if ever asked

what we meant by these, we'd say "mary, mary,"
like the saints we pretended
to wish to be. I never planned to make myself
the tragic one, to pass myself around and into

the soft and unkind hands of numb
and unkind men who never drew me into themselves
the way she drew a field of lilies with a single
embrace. She taught me, like a trumpet, to hum
and be still. We lined the baskets on the sill.

for Amanda

Self-Portrait as Vestal Virgin

I made you a promise I intended to keep:
that I'd cover my body, keep your words near
as the pearl at the curve of my ear.

Of the gull flying above the ocean's deep
belly I thought, *he has nothing to forgive, nothing to fear.*
Still, I made you a promise I intended to keep.

And from the fish below, daring to leap
toward the threat of a beak—I heard
desire sigh like a pearl at the curve of my ear.

Instinctively, I waited until the seeping
light of day to wear a dress I hadn't planned to wear,
unmake the promise I intended to keep.

When I undressed before him, underripe
like new fruit, I imagined you there,
saying: *you made me a promise you intended to keep,*
then buried it like a seed in the curve of a pear.

What God and My Mother Have in Common

My mother sees the red racecar
on my sixth-grade Valentine—

my heart is racing for you

—the scraps of which
even a mechanic
couldn't put back together.

My mother sees the hair
go missing from my legs.
She reaches
for the smooth new
animal of them
while she drives.

My mother haunts
every Ouija board
at friends' parties,
where she also stars
in every R-rated movie
and watches me
watch her.

My mother sees the empty
glass bottles
in the black bag
in the white bag
in the trash can
beside the curb.

And all the fingertips
and all the shoulders
and all the lips
I have touched

willingly or not.
She sees,

if not the pills,
then what the pills do.

But the thing that is killing me—
my mother doesn't see it.

II.

My Mother Tries to Teach Me About Cars

"If a man offers to help you
carry something heavy to your car
flex your biceps and say *no thanks.*

If a man pulls up next to you in his car
and gives you a thumbs-up
a holler   a compliment   a grunt
flip him the bird and keep running.

If a man pulls up next to you in his car
pants unzipped and hand jouncing
fly like a bird in the other direction.

If a man asks for directions
tell him to get lost.

If a man asks you to smile
bare your teeth.

If a man does not ask.
If a man demands.
If a man uses his hands
to demand. If it is
too late to run
to fly   to speak   to bare

be a wrench
against his mouth."

If I had a poem for every time a man—

then I would have as many poems
as gulls circling the bay,
landing like a fistful of breadcrumbs
just released—

and I would have a poem
instead of a man
circling me in his truck,
hollering as he speeds on

home to the promise
of breaded chicken
and his wife, whom, with his sudden
arrival, he plans to surprise—

At 22, I Can't Save the World

but I can smile
until loving me is as easy
as loving the ocean:
predictable in the rhythms
of its loneliness. More obedient to men
than moons, I can make myself a dog
and find someone to come to
when called, or to show up at his door
in a shade of lipstick that reminds him
of mortality. I can quiet myself
long enough to be the one
he'll sleep next to for a year
in his garage apartment, termite dust
powdering my hair like snow
in my far-away hometown.

After Watching *The Quiet Man*

I remember little else
but the fear that turns M.'s eyes
to moonstones. The dark room
and the wind that keeps forcing
the door open.

*

Once, a man walked into me
like a room. The colorless moon
in my single window
reminded him of loneliness.

*

In E.'s dreams of our future,
we drink martinis all afternoon
and the pearl ring on my left
hand clinks against the glass.

*

How S. twists M.'s hand behind
her back and forces his mouth
onto her bolted mouth.

*

Once, I was the window
a man looked through, saw the moon
and thought: *you look lonely tonight.*

*

In E.'s dreams of our future,
we share a room
with two single beds.

*

Like M., I have been known
to make myself so convincing
a ghost as to scream at the sight
of my own reflection.

*

Once, when my loneliness was
as large as the moon, I let a man
walk me into a windowless room.

*

In E.'s dreams of the future,
a man can consummate
his marriage whenever he desires.

*

How to explain why, before
she goes, M. turns to give S.
a quick kiss?

*

How to forgive the lies
left unspoken in those rooms?
More than once I kissed
a lonely man because he said
he could not forget the moon
in my hair.

What I Didn't Know at 23

When he came along preaching
all the good news he could
deliver me, I said yes

to his leather saddlebags
and yes to his Blessed Virgin
tattoo. I said yes to his dark

wine and his clever tongue.
I was taught to pray
for my enemies long before

I had any notion of one,
so when he came along
I didn't recognize the difference

between a coiled snake and a halo.
I was never taught to pray
for useful things—how to stop

a man from driving you drunk
or licking all the sweetness
from your mouth, promising diamonds

when your hands are full of glass.

Recluse

I will learn to survive this place: to lie
still in a room without windows and wait
for tornadoes to pass, to breathe the pine-
thick air, which, like loneliness, bears
its own close weight.
I will learn to survive the venomous
spiders that nest in the crooks of my house.
To survive the one who knocks on my door
until I agree to let him in, let him lay
the traps, sticky like rosin on the bows of his hands.

My Mother Tries to Teach Me How to Pray

When I fold my hands together, I don't think of
my childhood bedtime ritual: doubling my small

body under yours to kneel where you were kneeling,
asking the Lord that we might live another day. When

I fold my hands together, I don't think of you, but of
an almost-lover who folded sheets of paper into birds.

Dear dove, he'd say, kneeling beside me as I closed
my eyes to stars and let him bend me into the poems

he tucked inside his pocket. Unlike other mothers, you
never asked me to close my eyes when I prayed.

Even then you must have known the fear I had—not
of darkness—but of sudden light, the knowledge that

everything is made to disappear. When I kneel, I think
of begging for my life, have learned to call this prayer.

When I Don't Feel Like Taking the Lord's Name in Vain, I Say His

After Allison Seay

It was a broken egg with a neat sunshine yolk
it was new life in the figurative sense
& before this new life was resignation
& before resignation resentment
& a fight, the worst kind: a fight between me
& myself in a mirror trying to see
my face with his eyes
& wondering what he could have seen
—an apology is not *yes*—
before this fight was another kind of fight
a fight of bodies we do not speak of
but in this fight, I was a dog
at the foot of his bed
& I was ugly milky eyes
knotted fur I was a dress
ripped in the figurative sense petals
from he loves me/he loves me not flowers
before the fight I lost
& apologized for
losing there was something like confusion
which I mistook for happiness which I
mistook for pleasure the feeling of peeling
back layers of a corn husk to stroke
its golden hair but this was ignorance
& before this was another kind of ignorance
the ignorance of his very existence
& what I remember of this
I call silence

Another Summer Without Classical Music

I haven't lived in Southern California
very long but every summer
it occurs to me
after the summer has ended
that I should go see "Mozart
Under the Stars" or some other
classical music concert at the Hollywood Bowl
because I need to get out more
need to get more *culture*
at least that is what my lover tells me
but it occurs to me that I should tell him
that culture is not a bowl of spaghetti
or anything that can be twirled on a fork
and wiped up with a hunk of bread
then abandoned for days in the fridge
like most of the new plans I make—
canceled, because—as the actor
in my poetry workshop used to say:
we have a new realization every one to two seconds
and I'll believe just about anything
if it sounds interesting enough
which is why the only ghost I believe in
is that of a 1930s Hollywood actress
who jumped from the sign's *H*
and is sometimes seen wandering
below and maybe I believe this
because *H* is the letter I would choose
or because I don't trust the explanation
given for her death (learning her role
had been cut from her first film):
because *Thirteen Women* is about manipulating
women into killing themselves or one another

and now I have realized this too-easy coincidence
this culture I cannot digest
is proof that men have always wanted women
to hate women
so we will love them more

I Turn Away

After Fountain of Milk Spreading Itself
Uselessly on Three Shoes, *by Salvador Dalí*

Plump & improbable
as honeydew melons,
such breasts, in real life,
would topple the spire-waisted
girl beneath. As I consider
my own and refuse to make of them
some banal comparison to fruit,
I tell myself Dalí wasn't after
real life, then realize I've just
exonerated every man equally
undeserving of such forgiveness—
forgiveness being the lie I grant
when it is easier than remembering
that every man who has ever
seen my breasts has also seen,
felt, kissed, palmed
more than what his average hands
could hold. Every time I undress
before my lover, though he holds me
love-frozen in his eyes, I turn away
so as not to remind him.

Who Made Your Life a Living Bell

Once, I met a man who said my name
rang familiar. Every hour since,
I have heard an unwavering refusal
of emptiness—
the same note my mother held
calling me home from the dark.

III.

Fever Dream, or: My Mother Tries to Teach Me About Love

I awake in the damp orbit of what my body has made
& I'm a child again, sleepless beneath
a fever that clings to me like air—you're lifting
me out of bed & into the car & I'm lucid
with the stories you're telling me, or just

dreaming my memories—a car seat sliding
around the backseat of the Pinto you call
Old Girl—my arm busting through a coat sleeve
and coming loose as you pull it through—
feeling the air you make in your rush to where
I've fallen on the ice rink & the blade

of your skate as it cleaves my finger. You never
told me about the time you left. Why
you came back. I know love is a kind
of violence, a threatening grammar—how
a woman must love in spite of her body.

Other People's Apartments

It's not difficult to imagine that we could live
here, together, with the hanging plants,
Swedish soaps, strong water pressure.

At this confession, he turns toward
the wall's discerning arrangement of framed
maps and suggests we try locating ourselves,

our histories. *There we are*, I point to a shade of blue
that could be heaven—a betrayal
no less mundane than any of my others.

What is heaven but another word for
prison? The great gray mass of North America
reminds me of places I think I will not travel—

places that recall everything I know
and do not know about him. Us. I wonder
what use it will be, after I have died, to look back

on the map of my life. To see how many times
I was near to him and did not know it, and all
the times we might have saved each other.

The eye was not altogether unwelcome

The superstitious say
if you catch a dragonfly, you'll be married
within the year. Despite
my chasing, the girl I once was

feared dragonflies, each eye
the glass end of a kaleidoscope
refracting through her mind's
dark clouds. What glimmering
things her fingers had lifted
to places they did not belong!

I never thought
to be afraid of marriage—
the girl I once was
could wrap a white sheet
around her waist and pledge
her life to anything:
hamburger patty, I do,
frogs in the pond, I do—
saints in heaven, I do,
I do, I do.

It wasn't fear, but envy
I felt while watching
a dragonfly suspended
mid-air, so well
disguising its unrest.

The Day Before

A far-off scent of orange blossoms
retreating into buds. I didn't know
it then, this threading of arms
through first embrace,
but I felt some future forming
with the certain gentleness of a beast
eating from its person's hand.

Something Blue

The day we decide to marry,
B. gifts me a set of topaz earrings,
their luster like a promise I could keep.

Hours before I walk down the aisle,
my mother slips me a pair of earrings
—also teardrop, my birthstone—
she received the day I was born.

Like Themis or Justitia in a wedding dress,
I hold the sets, one in each hand.
Light scatters across the room.

Love has a way of felling the scales.
Why do I keep choosing her?

Love Poem with Iron and Stone

Maybe love is not
what lifts a man high above
your shoulders, spins him
like a rifle in a drill sergeant's
routine, or bends him willingly
as iron in your hands, the fire
you give so hot it leaves you
cold as the stone they say
you're made of. Or not,
when it's over, how you pull him
into the arch of your body,
almost enough to make him
disappear. Maybe

love is a way of forgetting.
Bending a shape
into an unfamiliar shape.
Breaking the links of a chain.
Maybe love is the bridge
you make of yourself
when you say *love is*
stronger than anything
because you and you alone
can endure the weight of an army
crossing the truss that is your body
without your heart,
that lonely muscle, giving way.

After Catie Rosemurgy

Self Portrait as Bonfire

The world is gone—all but stars enough
to know his body next to mine.
See how I love with my mind the wrist

that stokes the flames, wrests
branches from the fig-hearted tree,
unsheathes its shadows, mines

its ghosts. What I wouldn't do
to embrace him the way
fruit embraces its seed.

First Anniversary, with Tectonic Plates

Þingvellir, Iceland

Our bus driver says the Mid-Atlantic Rift
is the only place a human can stand

between two tectonic plates
and witness a million-years' process.

The country formed this way.
Lava fields rose to fill the rupture.

What kind of love is this—
when two things drift apart

but find a way to stay together? We
cross antiquity. He, asleep

in the seat beside me, unaware.

After Aimee Nezhukumatathil

Cuttings

In Hebrew, my name means favor, grace—
but I take more than I give. I idle
the mornings long after he goes and spend
the day buying plants to purify
the inside air. I pick ones called "mother
-in-law's tongue" or "viper's bowstring hemp"—
ones with the sharpest leaves. My life so far

is not without its edges. I have learned to make
myself dry to the touch, to ask for things
I do not need—steady light, an unobstructed
view. Evenings, I linger by the door
until he comes home, promise that tomorrow
I will try harder, will cede my barrenness,
even if I have to split myself in two.

My Mother Tries to Teach Me About Listening, or: Another Poem About Birds

I want to know the yellowthroat's quick trill
as it ricochets off my window, the song
she passes on to her young. I want to learn
birdsong, to identify a species from its call
and know whether, like a bird's, a child's voice
is a kind of aural fingerprint, unique in its demands
for Goldfish or the swing-push that would shatter
this barrier between earth and heaven.

Before you first strained your ears toward
the sound of my breathing and mothered the dark
night out of my lungs, before you memorized every
thorned and honeyed edge of my voice—
did you know you'd someday listen to a child's
voice and hear it otherworldly, learn it
well enough to paint its spectrogram by heart?

I Cannot Bury the Thought of [   ] Leaving

I want to talk about the name I chose
and how the pressure of each touch
becomes a fold in its impressionable

skin. The role I play in its shaping—
that every movement, my very density,
determines each arch, whorl. With this hand

I hold the string of grief's invisible kite.
How I carry the ghost of my love.
How I carry its flesh and its bone.

IV.

The Seafloor of Your Heart Sings Against It

Something left you late this morning,
so says the untwisting of small tracks.
Now you field-note what you're learning:
that whatever left you late this morning
came to make a fossil of its warning.
Yours is a loneliness that doubles back
like the animal that left you late this morning
& the twisting & untwisting of small tracks.

My Mother Tries to Teach Me About Grief

You never ask if I want the good
or the bad news first: you deliver

the bad with all the suddenness
of shattered glass, then sweep

what's left of it into a dustpan.
All luster, no light. I prefer

to stuff bad news into a weekend
bag among folds of zebra prints

and island botanicals—patterns so
distracting I almost forget the infinite

ways I'm already grieving you.

Mother, Language

North Forest Lights, Crystal Bridges Museum of Art

Sapling bases garlanded with blue
bulbs conjure mycorrhizal networks.
The forest shimmers with conversation.
To someone just passing through,
this might resemble art less than it does an expensive
Christmas installation: the kind one drives by
in their car and sets the radio to,
the kind with an electricity bill that would make

my mother convulse. My mother, who sets
the thermostat between sixty and sixty-three degrees
inside the cocoon of her New England winters,
whose hands purple, crack, and crust from cold.

Because cold hastens temper and forgiveness,
it's never long before we fight
and make up, her fingers warming the spaces
between my own. A throb of heartbeats in my palm.
This way I've memorized her knuckles, grooved
like antique knobs, thumbnail nacreous
from a childhood incident with the car door,
and callouses: language of the body's

tenderness. I shoot a silent video of the lights
to send her, uncertain what she'll see in it.
Watching it later, I notice that my finger has eclipsed
the camera's eye. That, and a faint
blue pulsing in the background.

Winter in California

and the lemons have returned.
I twist one over-
plump and golden from the tree,
remembering the childhood
friend I wanted to be just like, whose
unusualness I wished in every way to match.
Because lemons were her favorite food,
I made them mine.

(Once, while refusing to eat a dinner
my father had prepared, I imagined a heap
of lemon slices and went to bed hungry.)

I read somewhere, or maybe
my mother told me, that larger fruits
contain less flavor. It's hard to measure
bitterness. Maybe what she told me
was: lemons are a symbol for sadness, pain,

death. I have felt these things, have tasted
a lemon and known its sour,
let it teach me everything I have lost.

Spring in Mississippi

This time of year   the light bends like I do
hungering for a more infinite
dazzling life   I am trying to tell you
about the way things are   how like any-
thing   the magnolia blossoms into its own
abbreviated life   that the same
rain that makes it grow   also drenches it
to death   I am trying to tell you that
somehow   the rain always finds the most
vulnerable parts   and that the act of clearing
is a kind of violence   and that to love
is to believe in the adequacy
of lamplight   and its brightness on your palms

After Visiting Musée d'Orsay
on the Hottest Day in July

The intimacy I remember best from childhood
is my own tongue licking vagrant
sugar from the corners of my mouth.

I remember, too, the girl in the striped dress
in a large print of Renoir's *Dance at Le Moulin de la Galette*
above the fireplace we never lit. Sometimes, I wanted
to be her, to have that woman—that mother—
drape her determined arm around my shoulder.

I still know the girl's face well, how she evades
glances from a potential suitor
and avoids the viewer's eyes.

I wonder what hell she is trying to forget.

The average human brain weighs
three pounds: about the same
as a bag of apples or small potatoes.

Now, my mother's brain is that
minus a cup of sugar.

If the mind is its own place,
avoidance is the topography
my mother and I tread best.

The elephant grows lonelier each year.

I used to believe forgetting
could be a blessing.
Hearing her call out, again,
again to her dead,
I know it is not.

My Mother Tries to Teach Me How to Garden

On Saturdays we knelt, too—
I watched you make holes
in the unforgiving New England dirt,
then fill them with the seeds you carried
like Communion. I heard you pray
for cooperative weather, then confess
you were not a patient woman.

This must be why I first confused impatiens
with *hurrying*, with *impulsive*—unsurprisingly,
the root of impatiens does not wait—
the seed pods burst open if touched. The root
of garden is *enclosure*, and in this way, I became
like you—leaving home before the first
nodding buds of spring. I never

busied my hands with beauty—
instead, I taught myself to see
the fastened slip stitch of a flower's
anther to filament, the ghost apple
suspended long after the ice storm

departs. Here, in this small
southern town, so far from anything
I call home, a whole grove flourishes
within an abandoned building, restless
like a greenhouse that has shaken off its glass.

(Un)requited Love Poem

I love the one who sits alone
at the café's small table,

content to wait for no one
but the humming waitress

who comes to refill the glass.
I love the waitress's hands, how

they arranged the small yellow
flowers in the vase, and her

eyes, which saw what the hands
had done and thought it good.

I love the table, reclaimed
like a child who has wandered away

and then humbly returned. I love
the one who made the table,

who sanded and stained the wood.
I even love the one who chopped

the wood from the tree—
the tree I love most of all.

My Mother Tries to Teach Me About Transubstantiation

and I am only half-listening, too busy
holding my foot beneath the bathtub's

faucet, pretending I have, not a foot,
but a mermaid's tail. I try to tell you

that the water is too cold. Freezing.
You reach into the unexpected

heat, and for the first time, look
at me like I am the child I am.

I hadn't been trying to convince you
that cold and hot were the same—

I'd been trying, but had no words, to say
that the sensation of any two extremes is—

a burn is a burn, regardless of origin.
Take anything: God, god: the closer I get

to belief, the more it feels like unbelief.
Still, any word from you can undo me.

Don't you see how the more I become
myself, I become you? Do you feel it too?

NOTES

In "My Mother Tries to Teach Me About Language," the line "and cleans me from the inside out" is adapted from a line in Natasha Trethewey's "White Lies."

"Love Poem with Iron and Stone" is inspired by and borrows its first line from Catie Rosemurgy's "Love, with Trees and Lightning."

The title, "The eye was not altogether unwelcome," is a line in Jenny George's poem, "Vision."

ACKNOWLEDGMENTS

I would like to extend my gratitude to the editors and readers of the following publications, where versions of these poems first appeared:

The Best American Poetry Blog: "Another Summer Without Classical Music"

The Boiler Journal: "I Turn Away"; "The Sound"

Cream City Review: "My Mother Tries to Teach Me How to Garden"

EcoTheo Review: "My Mother Tries to Teach Me About Language"; "Winter in California"

Faultline: "What God and My Mother Have in Common"

Image: "My Mother Tries to Teach Me About the Body" and "Self-Portrait as Vestal Virgin"

Josephine Quarterly: "After Visiting Musée D'Orsay on the Hottest Day in July"

Lake Effect: "Mother Language"; "Love Poem with Iron and Stone"

The Missouri Review Poem of the Week: "When I Don't Feel Like Taking the Lord's Name in Vain, I Say His"

NELLE: "Cuttings" and "(Un)requited Love Poem"

Nimrod International Journal: "Bildungsroman"; "The Seafloor of Your Heart Sings Against It"; "My Mother Tries to Teach Me How to Pray"; "Realizations While Staying in Other People's Apartments"

Northwest Review: "At 22, I Can't Save the World" and "The eye was not altogether unwelcome"

The Penn Review: "My Mother Tries to Teach Me About Faith"

Raleigh Review: "After Watching *The Quiet Man*"

Rappahannock Review: "What I Didn't Know at 23"

RHINO: "My Mother Tries to Teach Me About Transubstantiation"

The Rumpus: "If I had a poem for every time a man—"

Shenandoah: "Fever Dream, or My Mother Tries to Teach Me About Love"

South Dakota Review: "I Cannot Bury the Thought of Your Leaving"

The Southern Review: "April in Mississippi"

Thuya Poetry Review: "My Mother Tries to Teach Me How to Draw"; "My Mother Tries to Teach Me About Grief"

Woodward Review: "Strange Penance" and "My Mother Tries to Teach Me About Listening, Or: Another Poem About Birds"

Yemassee: "My Mother Tries to Teach Me About Cars"

"My Mother Tries to Teach Me About Language" and "My Mother Tries to Teach Me How to Pray" also appeared in the *Mid/South Sonnets* Anthology (Belle Point Press, 2023).

I would also like to thank the writers whose own work and friendship have sustained me at any and all moments of this book's journey. The process of writing this collection would not have been the same (possible) without the kindness you've shown me along the way, whether you helped carve out space to publish my work, gave me incisive critique or editorial advice, listened to me vent or celebrate, or shared a meal or a cocktail and a conversation about writing: Brooke Harries and Lauren Swift, Taylor Bratches, Kaily Dorfman, Cassie Leone, Aaron Styza, Inez Tan, and Justine Yan. Jessica Guzman, Todd and Mary Osborne, Jon Riccio, Matthew Schmidt, Joseph Holt, Caleb Tankersley, Allison Campbell, Leah Beth and Sara Lewis, and Annette Boehm. Sarah Audsley, Liz Johnson, Michael Battisto, Courtney DuChene, Meredith Herndon, Caitlin Palmer, Rebecca Stoner, Kelly Grace Thomas, Natalie Staples, Sean Hooks, and C.T. Salazar.

With extra special gratitude for my poetry mentors, Angela Ball and Rebecca Morgan Frank, whose wisdom and generosity to me have proven endless. Morgan, you said to write the thing that scares you, and, well, here it is.

With genuine appreciation as well for the first readers of this manuscript, my MFA thesis advisors: Amy Gertsler, Michael Ryan, and Oren Isenberg.

I am indebted to the University of California-Irvine's MFA program for the time, support, and space to write the poems in this manuscript. I am also thankful for the support I've received from Missouri Southern State University to attend the Napa Valley Writers' Conference, where I experienced the joys of working with Jane Hirshfield and Victoria Chang and wrote the poems that rounded out this collection. To my colleagues and students at MSSU: you inspire me daily.

My sincerest gratitude to Dr. Ross Tangedal and the team at Cornerstone Press for making this journey to publication as smooth as possible.

My awe and appreciation belong to Lina Sadziuviene (https://www.saatchiart.com/linaartbox), whose exquisite piece, "Shades of Leaves," graces the book's cover. I am thrilled to share artistic space with you again.

To my best friends, not only in words but in life. Even from afar, you make me feel seen, cared for, and supported. TU4L.

To my family, especially my immediate: Mom, Dad, Timmy—I love you, you are everything.

Brady, I love you infinite dots and unlimited punctuation. Thank you for your patience, gentleness, support. May you never fall asleep on a tour bus again.

I believe all lives are worth writing about, but Mom, thank you for giving me mine. It's impossible to say how much you mean to me, but I'll keep trying.

Hannah Dow is the author of *Rosarium* (2018). Her poems have appeared in *Shenandoah, Image, The Southern Review, Pleiades, The Best American Poetry* blog, and elsewhere. She received the *Cream City Review* Summer Prize in Poetry, selected by Aimee Nezhukumatathil, as well as awards and scholarships from Bread Loaf Orion and the Sewanee Writers' Conference. Hannah lives in Bentonville, Arkansas, and is an Assistant Professor of English and creative writing at Missouri Southern State University.